I dedicate this book to my family and my law enforcement brothers and sisters.

Table of Contents

Contents

Preface:

Thank you for purchasing *How to Interact Safely with Law Enforcement: The Ultimate Guide to Understanding Police Culture, Traffic Stops, Arrests, and How to File Misconduct Complaints.* This book has been a project of mine for several years, and I hope it helps you understand the sometimes-intimidating experience of interacting with law enforcement. This book aims to give the reader an understanding of how law enforcement officers interact with citizens and how to navigate those encounters safely and proactively.

Before we get into the first chapter, let me introduce myself. My name is Timothy Weston. I am a lieutenant with a mid-sized police department in Texas. When writing this book, I served as a police officer in the State of Texas for 27 years. For 20 years, I worked in the Patrol Division of my department, serving as a patrol officer, patrol sergeant, and patrol lieutenant. As a supervisor, I managed hundreds of officers throughout my career and investigated many complaints of police misconduct. My current assignment is with my department's administrative division.

Police community relations are at an all-time low in America. Those of us who serve as law enforcement officers must be the ones to take the first steps toward repairing those damaged relationships. Perspective and communication are central to understanding each other. I hope this book contributes to the process of understanding between law enforcement professionals and the communities they serve.

While writing this book, I took the viewpoint of conversing with you, the reader. I intend to present easy-to-understand ways of navigating interactions with law enforcement officers while providing a balanced understanding of the law enforcement officer's viewpoint. By providing a balanced perspective, I hope we, as a society, can begin to heal past wounds and build a more meaningful future.

Lastly, accountability is the only answer to police misconduct and criminal behavior. Law enforcement officers are ordinary people with the same aspirations as everyone else. Overall, most police officers are good people. However, it is impossible to eliminate all bad actors within law enforcement. There will always be those who enter the occupation of law enforcement with malice in their hearts, and we, as professional law enforcement officers, must root out those individuals and expel them from our profession.

I hope you enjoy *How to Interact Safely with Law Enforcement: The Ultimate Guide to Understanding Police Culture, Traffic Stops, Arrests, and How to File Misconduct Complaints.* Please tell a friend or family member so others can benefit from this book.

Chapter 1 Law Enforcement Culture

The theme of this chapter is to give you a basic understanding of the law enforcement profession and its challenges today. It will:

- Help you understand how the training and indoctrination of law enforcement officers further shape the perspective of law enforcement officers.
- Open a window into law enforcement culture and its influences on the behavior of law enforcement officers.
- Describe how organizational structure affects the distribution of law enforcement resources in your community.

Agency size and type, law enforcement culture, organizational structure, and training of law enforcement officers are often very different from city to city, county to county, and state to state. Many states have adopted standardized training for licensing police officers and law enforcement professionals. Those standards of training usually encompass academy training and in-service training. The information provided in this book may not be an exact match for your location. Yet, it will generally explain how law enforcement organizations operate and how the officers in those agencies make decisions.

History:

Law enforcement has existed for over a hundred years in the United States.

For most of the 20th century, White males comprised the ranks of law enforcement officers. Formal rank structure, conformity, and a paramilitary mindset were standard in the profession. Law enforcement officers during this time viewed themselves as guardians of the social order, in addition to their responsibilities as law enforcement officers. The guardians of the social order perspective led to a patriarchal belief within American society that police officers were father figures and role models. The Baby Boomer generation most often identifies police officers in this manner. As time progressed, women began to enter the profession, along with minorities. This diversity led to a changing view of police officers, from father figures to community partners.

Since the second half of the 20th century (the 1950s to the 1990s), strong bonds of trust bound most law enforcement officers and the communities they served together. Unfortunately, On March 3rd, 1991, the Rodney King incident changed many Americans' views of law enforcement. The subsequent riots from that incident destroyed entire neighborhoods in Los Angeles and across the country. Trust in law enforcement continued to erode across the country as technology such as camcorders captured video and images of police officers unlawfully using force against their fellow citizens.

With the invention of the smartphone and its capability to capture high-quality video came a flood of videos that captured police misconduct.

Fast-forward to today, the recording of law enforcement officers is commonplace. In addition, many agencies require their officers to wear body cameras. When an officer makes a mistake, acts inappropriately, or engages in criminal behavior, those videos find their way to the internet.

Social media, video-sharing sites such as YouTube and Twitter, and traditional media companies feed the narrative that all police officers are corrupt or part of a systematic effort to suppress minorities.

Nothing could be further from the truth. Most cases of police misconduct result from poor training, lack of knowledge, bad management, and incompetent decision-making. Only a fraction of a percent results from intentional acts based on bias. Many of these individuals had problems before being hired and had numerous misconduct violations throughout their careers. Furthermore, in those few cases, we, as law enforcement officers, failed to root out those individuals and expel them from the profession.

Therefore, the distrust of police officers and law enforcement professionals is traceable to poor hiring practices, inadequate training, bad management, and a failure of accountability. Nevertheless, more than 800,000 sworn law enforcement officials are in the United States today. Most 800,000 sworn law enforcement officials are good people of every ethnicity, race, and gender. They are not perfect, and they make mistakes, so the tension between law enforcement and the citizens they serve still exists.

This tension causes distrust, apathy, false assumptions, and even violence. We must recognize that law enforcement professionals are neither robots nor infallible human beings to break down this tension. They are products of the training they receive, the general culture of law enforcement, and their agencies' organizational structure.

Joining the Profession:

When an individual decides to become a law enforcement professional, their perception of the career comes from movies, TV series, and interactions with law enforcement. Many law enforcement applicants believe they will enter the profession as a detective, undercover narcotics officer, or SWAT team leader. The reality is that all recruits work on patrol, answering calls for service and interacting with the public.

Before an individual becomes a law enforcement professional, they undergo a hiring process. The hiring process generally consists of an aptitude test, physical agility testing, background investigation, polygraph exam, and psychological exam. Some jurisdictions require drug testing and additional physical testing. The percentage of individuals who apply for a law enforcement job and make it through the selection process is less than ten percent.

The testing process identifies those who meet the minimum requirements and weeds out those who are not fit to serve. In general, the profession does an excellent job of finding the best applicants from the pool of applicants available. That is not to say that the best people become law enforcement officers. On the contrary, the selection process can only choose the best applicants from the pool available. The nationwide pool of applicants has dwindled considerably in the last five years. The negative perception of law enforcement officers, combined with low pay for the job performed, has created a perfect storm of low turnout for the profession. In some ways, this book is needed now more than ever because the number of qualified applicants has dropped, and thus the need for understanding becomes more urgent.

When a law enforcement recruit is hired, they often attend a traditional style of instruction called the Police Academy or academy training. Most states have a governmental body that sets the standards for the education of law enforcement officers. Regardless of the state, most modern academy training is several hundred to over a thousand hours. The training is primarily classroom instruction, followed by physical training (defensive tactics, arrest mechanics, restraint techniques). There is a considerable amount of time dedicated to firearms proficiency. During this academy training, police recruits experience law enforcement culture for the first time.

Law enforcement is a paramilitary profession. Rank structure and adherence to the orders of commanding officers become second nature to new police recruits from day one. Police recruits must meet grooming standards, wear a uniform, be punctual, follow orders, ethically conduct themselves, and accept the law enforcement culture.

I have mentioned law enforcement culture several times in this chapter, but I still need to define it. Let us explore the concept of law enforcement culture in more detail.

Police Culture:

Law enforcement culture is the belief in and understanding of the role of a law enforcement officer in society. This belief is a product of many generations of officers who passed on their views and ideas to the next generation. It is organic, meaning law enforcement culture is constantly changing and influenced by the part of the country you live in and the make-up of the people there.

In general, law enforcement culture consists of three common aspects:

1. Formal Rank Structure – Everyone knows their position and role
2. Warrior Mindset – Teaching law enforcement officers how to survive traumatic events
3. Loyalty – Loyalty to your fellow officers and the agency you serve

Rank Structure:

The formal rank structure varies from agency to agency but follows military-style ranks.

1. Officer – A sworn member of a police department or law enforcement agency
2. Corporal – Often a first-line supervisor with a small span of control
3. Sergeant – Also considered a first-line supervisor with a larger span of control
4. Lieutenant – Sometimes referred to as Watch Commanders; they will run a division or a shift
5. Captain – Often called Division Commanders or Precinct Chiefs; they are responsible for a large division or an entire precinct
6. Assistant Chief – Responsible for whole sections of an agency (operations, support services, etc.)
7. Chief – Chief executive law enforcement officer is usually appointed by a governmental body but can be elected in the case of sheriffs and constables

State law enforcement organizations use the ranks of Trooper, Major, Colonel, and General.

The rank structure is critical to understand because it gives perspective on how law enforcement officers view themselves. Your rank provides meaning, responsibility, and authority to every individual. Status and authority can sometimes consume officers, leading to rigid thinking and limited decision-making. Rank can also allow officers to shift responsibility by claiming they cannot make decisions or determine what to do without supervisor approval.

The most significant aspect of rank influencing law enforcement culture is the parallel with the military. This military style of thinking has led to the controversial warrior mindset. Training in the warrior mindset begins at the academy level and continues throughout a law enforcement officer's career. The warrior mindset mentally fortifies an officer to use deadly force to preserve his or her or another person's life. It dictates that the officer will do whatever it takes to survive a deadly force encounter. This mindset benefits most new police officers who seldom have experienced violence directed at them and come from middle-class backgrounds.

Warrior Mindset:

Many commentators and critics of law enforcement blame the warrior mindset for excessive force incidents. However, with the warrior mindset, it is easier to prepare the average police recruit to use deadly force against another person. Most police recruits have a romanticized view of good winning over evil. The reality is much different. The unpredictability of law enforcement demands that an officer expect the worst possible outcome.

I once had an instructor at an officer survival school who said, "be kind to everyone you meet, but have a plan to kill everyone to meet." He said that preparation for the worst, even in seemingly ordinary situations, is critical to surviving a traumatic event. I can attest to the unpredictability of critical incidents, specifically deadly force confrontations. They are rarely linear, highly chaotic, supercharged with emotion and fear, compounded by legal and procedural constraints, and never go according to plan. The mindset necessary to not only survive a traumatic event but also still be able to function and act decisively requires a law enforcement officer to focus on the goal of survival. Therefore, the dual-edged sword of a warrior's mindset enables officers to survive and function during a critical incident but also causes them to operate in a state of near-constant hyper-vigilance.

Officers in a near-constant state of hyper-vigilance often create tension in the communities they serve. Overly vigilant officers treat everyone as a threat and do not appropriately assess a low-threat situation. Victims of crime or low-level offenders often feel mistreated by overly vigilant law enforcement officers. During my career, I resolved numerous complaints of officers who were too vigilant for the circumstances. Being too vigilant makes citizens feel "they were the bad guy" when they report being a crime victim or committing a minor offense like running a stop sign.

Proportionality was always the key to resolving these types of complaints. I spent many hours teaching officers how to assess the threat level of a situation correctly while at the same time remaining vigilant but not overly so. In practice, it is a difficult skill to master. Law enforcement must address this issue at the academy and continuing education levels. Understanding how the warrior mindset and hyper-vigilance can lead to a dangerous escalation of tensions between officers and citizens provides a view into one of the most influential parts of the law enforcement culture.

Loyalty:

Unwavering loyalty has a significant impact on law enforcement culture. It binds people of every race, background, ethnicity, and gender and transcends political alignments. Loyalty within law enforcement is akin to the loyalty shared by military members and veterans. The best example of fellowship created by loyalty is how police officers from other states and other nations instantly experience a bond when they meet. Regardless of whom you work for (city, county, state, federal), mutual respect and an unspoken understanding of each other occur. There are no secret handshakes or code words exchanged. If you have ever done the job of law enforcement, it changes you in a way that members of law enforcement can recognize.

The level of loyalty described above is created early in a police recruit's career. It is cultivated in the academy and follows officers no matter their assignment.

Once officers form friendships, their bonds of loyalty are unwavering. Those loyalty bonds are cemented even further when officers share difficult or traumatic experiences. Who else can understand what you are going through after a traumatic event except for your fellow officer who was right there with you? Unfortunately, this high level of loyalty leads officers to believe they can only turn to their fellow officers for help. Although we have improved the availability of mental health services to officers in the last two decades, there is still much to improve.

Loyalty feeds into the hyper-vigilant state I mentioned earlier. Being loyal also means you will do whatever it takes to save a fellow officer's life because they will do the same for you. Staying vigilant ensures you can meet that obligation but can also cause you to see others (citizens or suspects) as threats.

Loyalty has its place. It enhances the willingness of an officer to enter dangerous situations he or she would otherwise be fearful of entering. Knowing that no matter what, your fellow officers are coming to back you up allows a law enforcement officer to respond to dangerous situations without paralyzing fear.

Formal rank structure, a warrior mindset, hyper-vigilance, and loyalty shape law enforcement culture, which instructs law enforcement officers how to act, whom to trust, and how to survive the stresses and trauma of the profession. Recognizing these fundamental aspects of law enforcement culture will give insight into how law enforcement officers view the world. This knowledge will empower you to identify the type of officer you encounter. It will also help you interact with them, resulting in a higher likelihood of a positive outcome.

Organizational Structure:

The organizational structure of law enforcement agencies varies significantly from state to state and region to region. However, it is vital to understand how your local law enforcement agency functions and how its culture influences the type of law enforcement your community will receive.

There are five types of law enforcement organizational structures:

1. Quality of Life
2. Traditional
3. Specialized
4. Metropolitan
5. Rural

Quality-of-life law enforcement agencies tend to be smaller departments of less than 20 sworn officers, typically forming in or around larger cities. They often adopt an identity or name that reflects the area's geography.

A quality-of-life law enforcement agency aims to provide the citizens of a city or township with a stable, predictable, status-quo lifestyle. These agencies focus on outsiders as the main threat and stress traffic enforcement, positive citizen interaction, and keeping crime very low or non-existent. Most of these agencies value the citizens of their community over those "who don't live here" and view their police department as almost personal security—some quality-of-life departments issue windshield stickers for the residents of the city or township. Most of these agencies are located in affluent areas but can also be in low-income neighborhoods.

Traditional law enforcement agencies make up the country's vast majority of organizations. These types of law enforcement agencies are reactionary to crime, often not proactive, adhere to a formal rank structure, and have deep bureaucracies. They range from mid-sized to large but could be more metropolitan-sized. Their focus is to aggressively target criminals, utilizing a zero-tolerance style of policing, with some agencies employing good community relations. They are often stuck in the past and resistant to change. In general, traditional law enforcement agencies are reliable partners to the communities they serve but rarely take responsibility for misconduct.

Specialized law enforcement agencies are often airport police departments, transit police departments, and school district police departments. These agencies have specific mission statements, which usually focus on a particular law enforcement goal. They often stress the security of locations or public transit (i.e., subways, buses, trains, and planes). They typically serve a transient population rather than an identifiable community. The role of their police officers is often limited and narrowly focused.

Metropolitan police departments are massive organizations found in major U.S. cities like New York, Chicago, Houston, Los Angeles, and Dallas. Employing thousands or tens of thousands of officers is common among these agencies. Additionally, large complex bureaucracies staffed by civilians and sworn personnel can make navigating these agencies challenging for the citizens they serve. A central headquarters is typical among metropolitan agencies, accompanied by numerous decentralized precincts to manage a large geographic area.

Rural law enforcement agencies are often located in the heartland of the U.S. They are typically sheriff's departments but can also be smaller police agencies. The chief law enforcement officer at a sheriff's department is an elected official who will oversee deputies and the county jail system. Rural agencies have low staff numbers and share some common traits with quality-of-life departments. Maintaining the status quo is their primary mission. However, rural law enforcement agencies have been on the front lines of confronting the methamphetamine and opioid epidemics in the last two decades.

Chapter 2 Types of Officers & Traffic Stops

Combining the knowledge of law enforcement culture with organizational structure paints a picture of the average officer's perspective as they go about their day-to-day duties. However, understanding the types of officers, you may encounter will enhance your ability to interact with a law enforcement officer.

Types of Officers

Generally, law enforcement officers fall into four categories.

1. Rookies
2. Veterans
3. Aggressive
4. Drones

Officers come in all shapes, sizes, genders, races, and backgrounds. You can find officers from NYPD to the smallest agencies that fit the above categories. Each of these categories of officers has its unique aspects. Understanding those distinctive qualities will help you identify the type of officer you might encounter and form the basis of this chapter's discussion on communicating with them and having a positive encounter.

Rookies tend to be new officers to the profession of law enforcement but are not always young in age. For example, you could be 40 years of age and be a rookie if you just entered the profession. Every law enforcement officer starts his or her career as a rookie. Law enforcement is an experienced-based profession, and it takes time for new officers to learn the job. Usually, it takes two to three years to move beyond the rookie stage. During that time, rookies make mistakes and often need more supervision than tenured law enforcement officers need. Rookie officers - often called unguided missiles - can be erratic in how they work. An unguided missile can hit the target and make a difference but often fall short. There is nothing wrong with being a rookie officer; failure is the greatest teacher, so learning from minor mistakes is part of the learning process. That is not to say that rookie officers are not accountable for their actions; they need accountability and often need good mentors to guide their progress.

Rookie officers tend to have a change the world attitude. They want to make a difference. Some want to make a name for themselves. They chase the big drug bust or try to find the most wanted person in their jurisdiction. They often spend their entire shift trying to locate stolen vehicles because doing so can lead to a police chase. They also crave excitement.

On a side note, when I was a rookie, a veteran officer once told me police work is 90 percent paperwork and ten percent excitement. It takes a little while for most rookies to realize that once the excitement is over, then the hours of paperwork begin. It is worth it for many rookies, but eventually, they learn to manage the need for excitement with the amount of paperwork they have to do.

If you encounter a rookie law enforcement officer, they are most likely just as nervous as you are, if not more so. They tend to want to do everything right, making them shortsighted and only able to focus on one thing at a time. Be patient, it may take them a little longer to finish the job, but they will get there. Rookies sometimes suffer from a lack of empathy. They habitually see the law as black and white when every situation is unique, and not all circumstances require law enforcement action. Mentors play a prominent role in moving rookies away from the mindset that everyone gets a ticket or goes to jail. Unfortunately, many departments do not have a mentor program, and rookie officers are left to try to navigate their first few years independently. Remember, just like new doctors, lawyers, nurses, and truck drivers, no one enters the law enforcement profession knowing what to do in every circumstance. Even the most senior law enforcement officers can make a rookie mistake.

Veterans are highly experienced, giving them a higher competency level. They also understand the stress of the job. They tend to have good decision-making skills and good threat identification skills. Moreover, veterans intuitively understand the profession's dangers, allowing them to react quickly and decisively. Most veterans understand that people fall on hard times and make mistakes. They express empathy better than rookie officers but know when to put those feelings aside and get the job done. A veteran will listen to your story, assess its relevance to the situation, and take the appropriate action.

Veterans suffer from burnout, which is common in the profession. Veterans with burnout can seem indifferent. They also can display a callous attitude towards the emotions of others. Indifference and a callus attitude are often a result of repeated exposure to emotional trauma. Veterans see the horrific aftermath of suicides, homicides, assaults, tragic accidents, and injury or death of children. No matter how strong of a person you are, repeated exposure to traumatic events scars you. The result is a numbing effect that many veteran officers report after years of service. In a way, this numbing effect is a defense mechanism against repeated emotional trauma. Unfortunately, it can give the appearance of indifference.

Veterans are more likely to admit their faults and seek mental health services. Veterans make better decisions than most rookies make but make mistakes as well. They often have a good attitude and a professional demeanor and will do the job efficiently.

Aggressive law enforcement officers can be at any point in their career (rookie or veteran). A sense of right drives this type of officer, and they tend to view enforcement action as a means to an end. For example, an aggressive law enforcement officer will target a known criminal and repeatedly conduct traffic stops for minor infractions on the known criminal's vehicle. These actions pressure the criminal to leave the area or end up in prison. Some might say this is a good tactic, but the problem is that sometimes there is no known criminal to target, and the aggressive officer – who only knows one way to deal with people – uses the same tactics on non-repeat offenders. The average citizen does not need this level of intrusion to correct a minor traffic violation. Therefore, aggressive officers will request assignments in high-crime areas because every traffic stop or investigation will likely involve known criminals or known associates of criminals. Again, this leads to complaints from innocent citizens who feel threatened by an aggressive officer who only sees citizens as potential offenders.

Aggressive law enforcement officers do serve a purpose. They thrive in high-stress situations. They usually maintain a high physical fitness level. They are relentless against offenders who bully and harm others. Their sense of right and wrong drives them to make a criminal's life difficult. Like rookie officers, aggressive officers need a target, direction, additional supervision, and, most importantly, mentors to help them learn how to balance their approach to law enforcement.

Lastly, aggressive law enforcement officers hate to lose. In law enforcement, the suspect wins more often than you would think. Suspects evade detection, have others take the fall for them, get off on a technicality, get probation or suspended sentences for serious crimes, and are released on bail for violent offenses. Aggressive law enforcement officers feel a moral obligation to right those perceived wrongs. That moral obligation leads a small percentage of aggressive officers to engage in noble corruption. Noble corruption in these circumstances is not theft of drug proceeds or assaulting a domestic abuser. It comes in the form of violating the suspect's civil rights. Those civil rights violations are fourth amendment violations and manipulating evidence to suit a preferred outcome. Some officers believe they are noble in violating the law because the suspect is a bad person, and the system protects suspects more than the victim. On a philosophical level, that belief can be persuasive. However, there is no place for noble corruption in law enforcement. Over the years, I have told aggressive officers, "sometimes suspects win, and sometimes they lose, but integrity is all that separates you from being a criminal."

Drones are long-serving law enforcement officers who have taken a passive approach to law enforcement. Their peers view them as retired on duty, doing time, or counting the days until retirement.

Drones, like rookies, veterans, and aggressive officers, have a place in law enforcement. When the rookie and aggressive officers are busy booking suspects into jail or writing their arrest reports, someone has to answer the calls for service. Drone officers do not get in a hurry to go to calls. Drones will wait for backup before entering a dangerous situation, do not engage in proactive policing unless ordered, and often feel little sympathy for victims of non-violent crimes.

Drones generally take pride in writing a good report. Drones sometimes like to specialize in something they are interested in, such as collecting fingerprints at crime scenes, taking crime scene photos, looking for altered V.I.N. numbers on vehicles, and locating missing children. All these skills make a difference, but it is more of a behind-the-scenes difference.

If you are a victim of a property crime, violent crime, or fraud victim, a drone is whom you want to take your report. They tend to write good reports, have good attention to detail, and communicate well with citizens.

Now that we have discussed the categories of officers you may encounter, discussing what you can do when you come across these categories of officers is necessary.

Rookies: When encountering a rookie officer, try to understand that they are new and maybe nervous. The profession of law enforcement is experience-based and takes time to learn. Linear thinking can sometimes bog them down, so give them time to process the situation. Be respectful and pay them a compliment or two. At this point in their careers, they seek praise from their peers, supervisors, and the public. A little honey goes a long way with rookies.

Veterans: If you come across a veteran officer, they know what they are doing, will treat you like you treat them, and can sometimes seem callous in emotional situations. Veteran officers take pride in their work and tend to be methodical. They are more likely to conduct follow-up investigations. Veterans know the profession is a marathon, not a sprint. They do not seek praise as a rookie does, but a thank you can go a long way. I recommend getting to know the veteran officers in your area. They have a wealth of knowledge and good communication skills. Veteran officers will listen to you, consider your side of the situation, make a decision based on the evidence, and do their job. Treat a veteran officer will respect, and they will treat you likewise.

Aggressive: Aggressive officers focus better than rookie officers do. They tend to target criminals relentlessly but only know one speed. They focus on the public without a criminal to target, which tends to result in complaints. If you encounter an aggressive officer, stay calm and do not escalate the situation by arguing; if they treat you poorly, file a complaint and recommend that they work in a high-crime area. They are prone to noble corruption.

Drones: Drones are the exact opposite of rookie and aggressive officers. They take a passive approach to law enforcement. They do not get in a hurry, are not looking for excitement, and only want to do their time until retirement. Drones write good reports, tend to specialize, and move at a slower pace than rookies, aggressive, or veteran officers. You will most likely encounter a drone officer if you are a victim of a crime instead of during a traffic stop. Give them space and let them do their job at their speed. Like some nurses and doctors, they may have a poor bedside manner, but their work product is good. Complementing a drone officer may have the opposite effect than intended. Find out who their supervisor is and pay them a compliment in that manner.

The most common enforcement action the average citizen will experience is a traffic stop for a minor violation. It is an inconvenience, often nerve-wracking, scary, and confusing for most people.

Conversely, for the law enforcement officer, a traffic stop is one of the most high-risk law enforcement actions they can undertake. In training, every aspect of the traffic stop is broken down, which increases the likelihood of the officer surviving a deadly force encounter. When discussing this topic, it is vital to have the perspective of both the law enforcement officer and the citizen.

Before we get into the details of traffic stops, it is essential to remember the following; the side of the road is not a courtroom and is the worst place to argue over an officer's actions.

With that idea in mind, let us discuss traffic stops and how to navigate them.

Traffic Stops:

The traffic laws of every state allow law enforcement officers to detain a person who has committed a traffic violation, verify their driving eligibility, verify insurance, and confirm that the vehicle registration is current.

The necessary proof to conduct a traffic stop in most states is probable cause. There is no universally accepted definition of probable cause. Generally, law enforcement officers are taught that probable cause is evidence you can see or detect with your senses that would lead a reasonable person to conclude that a crime has been committed or was about to be committed.

The proof required for a criminal conviction – even a minor traffic violation – must be beyond a reasonable doubt and can only be determined in a court at a jury or bench trial.

Every state has laws allowing drivers who commit minor traffic violations to sign a ticket instead of appearing before a judge at the time of the offense. When you sign a ticket or citation, you receive a personal recognizance bond, which is your promise to appear or contact the court of jurisdiction.

It is essential to understand how a personal recognizance bond works. It keeps traffic stops short and grants citizens the freedom to address the violation at a time in the future. Without the P.R. bond, every person charged with a traffic violation must appear immediately before a judge. As you can imagine, that would be very inconvenient and unrealistic.

Here are some common sense things you should know and practice if a law enforcement officer stops you.

1. Stay calm – do not move around a lot or become angry or animated
2. Don't argue – trying your case on the side of the road will not change the outcome
3. Avoid accusations – Accusing the officer of racial bias or profiling during a traffic stop is pointless.
4. Sign the ticket or citation – the P.R. bond is designed to allow you the freedom to address the charges another day. Use this right to get out of the traffic stop quickly. In some jurisdictions, refusing to sign a citation or ticket can result in your arrest.

The Stop:

Generally, a traffic stop will follow the following format:

1. The initial stop
2. The approach (driver-side or passenger-side)
3. Initial contact
    a. Introduction
    b. The reason you were stopped
    c. Request for documents – driver's license, operator's license, insurance, registration
    d. Q&A – what might be causing the violations (medical emergency, distraction in the vehicle, something traumatic just occurred)
    e. Officer returns to the police vehicle
    f. Status check - warrant checks, driver's license checks, insurance validation, registration verification
    g. Outcome determination (verbal warning, written warning, citation, or arrest)
4. Secondary contact
    a. Issuing the citation
    b. Q&A
    a. End of the Stop

Before we get into the details, here are some suggestions to consider.

Remember the following acronym if a law enforcement officer pulls you over:

P.A.S. – Protocol©

P – Pull to the right and stop (stay in your vehicle unless directed out by the officer)

A – Avoid confrontation, don't argue, insult, or accuse, and stay polite

S – Sign the citation or ticket to end the traffic stop quickly

Every state in the U.S. has laws that govern a driver's responsibility when an emergency vehicle attempts to pass another vehicle or pull the driver over. Moving to the right and stopping are required in almost every version of those laws.

Once you pull over and stop your vehicle, refrain from moving around a lot or in an unusual manner. Officers are trained to observe the driver and occupants of vehicles they have stopped to detect furtive movements. Furtive movements can be:

- Reaching under the driver's seat or any other seat in the vehicle
- Opening the glove box
- Opening a center console
- Any abnormal action – pounding the steering wheel, yelling, throwing things, or getting out of the vehicle.

What we are discussing at this point is basic de-escalation tactics.

Every aggressive action you take, any furtive movements you make, or arguments you make during a traffic stop escalate the situation. The officer is already in a heightened state of alert because of the inherent danger of traffic stops, so stay calm and do not make the situation worse.

The potential for arrest and use of force increases rapidly when citizens become aggressive with a law enforcement officer who has stopped them. Officers will try to de-escalate situations but will take control of a situation before it gets out of hand.

In most states, law enforcement officers must use body-worn cameras and have an in-car video system recording during traffic stops. These video systems capture the officers' and your actions.

I can verify that many individuals who went to court contesting a traffic violation were later embarrassed and convicted when the jury saw their bad behavior on video. Most juries are sympathetic to defendants in traffic cases and give them the benefit of the doubt or lower fines. However, a jury will quickly assess the maximum penalty when the defendant's actions are out of line or rude. Do not be that defendant.

The Approach:

Before the officer approaches your vehicle, they will call in the location of the stop or G.P.S. location and log your vehicle's license plate.

The initial approach of a suspect vehicle is one of the most dangerous moments of a traffic stop. That is because the space between your vehicle and the police vehicle is no man's land. It is referred to in this manner because there is no cover available in that area, and the officer is at a distinct disadvantage because they cannot see into your vehicle well.

Again, stay calm, and keep your hands visible. Do not move around or start reaching for something in the vehicle.

The Initial Contact:

When the officer gets to your vehicle, they may stop or pause and touch the trunk area of your vehicle. This is normal. Officers are conducting this check to detect an ambush. In the academy and officer survival training, officers receive instruction about the dangers of ambushes from suspects hiding in the trunk of a vehicle.

At this point, there are two schools of thought.

One is the direct driver approach – the officer speaking with you at the driver's door.

The second is the passenger-side approach – where the officer interacts with you through the passenger-side window.

Both of these approaches have their place and serve a purpose.

A passenger-side approach is appropriate when traffic flows too closely to the driver's side of the vehicle, such as on a highway or interstate.

The driver-side approach is the most common practice in traffic stops.

Regardless of the approach (drive-side or passenger-side), how you interact with the officer is crucial to the overall outcome of the traffic stop.

Following the **P.A.S. Protocol©**, utilizing the A – avoiding confrontation is critical to setting the tone of the traffic stop. Remember, the officer is recording you, so even if the officer is rude, out of line, or aggressive, staying calm will only highlight their unprofessional behavior.

Introduction:

The officer will identify themselves to you. For example, hello, I am ____________, with ____________ department or agency. Some officers will use their rank if they have any in the introduction, such as sergeant, lieutenant, etc.

The Reason for The Stop:

The officer will inform you of the reason or reasons for the stop. For example, I stopped you today because you were speeding. I checked your speed using radar, indicating you were traveling 45MPH in a 35MPH zone.

At this point, some drivers decide to argue about the charge, how the officer determined the violation, or make accusations of racial bias or profiling.

Making that choice will not change the outcome or convince the officer they have made a mistake or violated your rights.

Most officers have not decided what enforcement action to take until they speak with you and assess the situation. Your chance of receiving a warning increases if you are respectful and non-confrontational. It is not a guarantee, but your chances go to about zero of a warning if you argue, are disrespectful, or accuse the officer of bias.

If you do not agree with the citation or violation alleged by the officer who stopped you, you have two options:

1. *Go to court and fight the charge:* If you receive a citation or traffic ticket, you have all the due process rights that every defendant has. You can plead not guilty. Request a jury or bench trial (a judge determines your guilt). You can defend yourself or hire an attorney to defend you. You have a right to face your accuser (call witnesses or question the officer who issued you a citation). You can present evidence that supports your innocence. You can appeal to the jury or judge for mercy.

2. *File a complaint against the officer:* You can file a complaint against the officer who stopped you with their agency or office assigned to investigate complaints (Internal Affairs, Professional Standards, or Office of Accountability). I will go more into depth in the chapter about complaints.

Nowhere in those two options did you see arguing or confronting the officer who stopped you as an option. Doing those things will ensure you receive a citation and cannot convince the officer you deserve a warning.

Request for Documents:

The officer will ask for your driver's license, proof of insurance, and or current registration. Depending on your state, you may have to produce additional documents.

Regardless, if you need to reach into a glove box, center console, purse, backpack, or luggage, tell the officer what you are about to do and get their permission to go into those areas. If you do not have the requested items, tell the officer you do not. In most cases, your driver's license can be looked up in a state database, your insurance can be identified in a similar database, and registration can be confirmed in another state database.

Q&A:

Most officers will ask questions of the driver at this point. Some may ask questions during the introduction phase, which is less common.

I always made it a point to ask, "Is there some reason why you were speeding today," or "is there a reason why your registration is expired." Sometimes, a driver would respond with a legitimate reason for their speed, such as a medical emergency or a family member being involved in an accident. However, I always verified with the hospital they were responding to or confirmed the accident was genuine and their family member was expecting them. If the driver lied, I mailed a citation to them.

The question-and-answer point of the traffic stop is where the situation can transition from a traffic violation stop to an investigatory stop.

The best example of this concept is driving while intoxicated or driving under the influence. During a traffic stop, if the officer smells alcohol on your breath, they begin a D.W.I. or D.U.I. investigation unrelated to the reason for the stop.

If the traffic stop transitions into a criminal investigation for something other than the traffic violation, you should still use the **P.A.S. Protocol©**.

At the end of this chapter, I will discuss pretext stops, investigatory stops, and criminal interdiction stops.

Officer Returns to the Police Vehicle:

This phase of the stop is the reverse of the approach, except the heightened awareness of the officer is still present because they are re-entering no man's land and are on the lookout for an ambush. Do not get out of your vehicle. If you locate a document or item the officer requested before returning to their vehicle, hold it out the window in your left hand. Let the officer approach you to get those items.

The same rules about furtive movements apply during this point in the stop.

On more than a few occasions in my career, this was the point where the driver decided to use their cell phone to call their relatives or friends and tell them about the traffic stop. As you can imagine, family members quickly assume the worst and want to rescue their child, spouse, mother, father, nephew, niece, uncle, or aunt.

It is incredibly dangerous to call individuals to an ongoing traffic stop. Again, the traffic stop is a high-alert situation for an officer. Calling individuals to the scene of a traffic stop is irresponsible and can lead to the arrest of those individuals if they interfere with an officer's official duties.

The best decision is to wait until after the traffic stop and then notify your family or friends.

Status Check:

This is the point in the stop where the officer will verify that your driver's license is not suspended, expired, or revoked. The officer will also check you through your state's wanted person and national wanted person databases. Insurance on your vehicle goes through a review process at this point. Verifying your vehicle's registration through your state's D.M.V database is also common. Some jurisdictions have additional databases, such as a local wanted database (local warrants for traffic tickets) or may have a wanted for questioning database.

The vast majority of people stopped for a traffic violation have a valid driver's license, are not wanted, have current insurance, and their registration is up to date.

An arrest will occur if the officer finds a warrant or warrants for your arrest. I will talk about arrests in another chapter.

If your driver's license is suspended, expired, or revoked, an arrest is possible; it depends on the laws in your state.

Expired insurance, no insurance, expired registration, or no registration may or may not result in your arrest. In most states, you will receive a citation for those violations.

Outcome Determination:

If all the status checks are clear (meaning no outstanding warrants and your driver's license is valid), the officer will decide if they will issue you a citation, ticket, or warning.

I utilized a review process to determine what type of enforcement action I took. Many officers use similar review processes. Here is an example of a review process:

1. **Level of Violation** – How far over the limit you were speeding or how long your equipment violations remained unresolved was part of the review process. I used ten over the speed limit to determine severity, which increased based on how many M.P.H. over the speed limit you were. For example, 35MPH in a 20MPH school zone = 15 M.P.H. over the speed limit and significantly increased the danger to children in the area.

2. **Your Demeanor** – This was a serious consideration for many officers who shared their review process with me. If you were ten over the speed limit but were respectful and had a clean driving record, I would give you a warning nine times out of ten unless you had a bad driving history or were a known criminal.

3. **Driving Record** – Your driving history tells an officer a lot about how you view the rules of the road and the consideration for the safety of

others. If, for example, you have a history of speeding, accidents, suspensions, reckless driving, racing, or no insurance, then the probability of a citation increases.

4. **Criminality** – Here is a reality check, if you are a known criminal, criminal associate, gang member, etc., do not expect any breaks. Contrary to popular belief, being a criminal is not a protected status. Deciding to engage in crime is a choice, and choices have consequences. With that being said, if you do not have a criminal record, that can influence an officer's decision to issue a warning.

It is important to remember that the above example of my and other officers' review processes is not definitive. Some officers will write a citation for any level of violation regardless of the circumstances. Sometimes, officers are assigned an enforcement area due to complaints of speeding, running stop signs, disregarding stop lights, accidents, or reckless driving. Officers assigned to an enforcement area or complaint zone will issue everyone a citation.

Many times in my career, I worked in an enforcement zone with the direction to reduce a specific type of behavior, driving, or violation. However, when I stopped people in an enforcement zone, I always took the time to explain what I was doing and why. I felt I owed it to the citizens I stopped to tell them why I was not going easy on them.

Secondary Contact:

When the officer returns to your vehicle, continue to utilize the A (avoid confrontation) part of the **P.A.S. Protocol©**. Stay calm. Stay polite and respectful even if you are angry about receiving a citation. Answer the officer's questions if they have any, which usually involves identifiers. The officer may ask to verify your address, place of employment, home phone number, work phone number, etc.

Lastly, utilize the S (sign) part of the **P.A.S Protocol©** and sign the citation. Numerous internet strategies recommend you refuse to sign, sign with a different name, or even demand to be brought before a judge immediately. None of the people who recommend these strategies will bail you out of jail, pay your fines, represent you in court, or be there when you try these ideas.

The quickest way to end the traffic stop and get back to your life is to sign your legal name, and then you can decide what to do without the stress of the traffic stop influencing you.

You will receive some form of receipt of the ticket, with information about where to go, whom to contact, etc. You can ask the officer questions now, but remember you are prolonging the situation.

The officer may ask you questions, such as do you have any questions. Do you know where the court is, etc.?

End of The Stop:

At this point, you and the officer part ways. Regardless of the outcome, remember that the officer's body camera and in-car camera system will still be recording. Do not make the mistake of burning rubber, shooting the officer the bird, or yelling obscenities.

Drive off carefully to avoid an accident, and determine how to proceed in a day or two when you can think clearly.

Final Thoughts on Traffic Stops:

Daily, we are reminded how quickly traffic stops turn into tragic events. Citizens and officers are both victims of these tragedies. Regardless of your perspective, the officer and the citizen are responsible for de-escalating their behavior during traffic stops.

We all need to take a moment to look at these tragedies from a 10,000-foot perspective.

The officer cannot assume everything will be fine because sometimes it is not. The citizen may have preconceived ideas about the officer's intent or judgment.

The officer is nervous and on a heightened state of alert because of the danger associated with stopping a vehicle. The citizen is often just as worried but needs clarification about what to do as well.

Arguments or aggressive actions by the officer or the citizen only escalate tensions and can lead to miscalculations.

Too often, officers find themselves in deadly force situations because the person they stop is in crisis and cannot cope, and the traffic stop is the catalyst that drives them to violence.

If I can leave you with a thought, it would be this; no matter how angry you are about a traffic stop, ticket, or even an arrest, ask yourself this question.

Is it worth your life?

The answer is always no.

No ticket or arrest is worth your life. Your friends and family need you more than you realize.

Remember the **P.A.S. Protocol©**; it can save your life.

Pretext Stops:

A pretext stop is a traffic stop, usually for a minor traffic violation (the pretext), but the officer intends to investigate another crime. Pretext stops help officers investigate drug crimes and suspicious activity, suppress gang activity, and pressure criminals to move out of an area.

Pretext stops are controversial. Some jurisdictions have outlawed them. I have utilized pretext stops in my career. Here is an example of how they are used.

An officer is watching a known drug house (crack house, meth house, dope house); when a vehicle pulls up, the driver gets out, goes inside, stays a few minutes, comes out, and gets back into the vehicle. When the vehicle pulls away from the curb, it fails to signal intent to re-enter the roadway. This traffic violation is minor but still a violation.

The officer follows the vehicle for a few blocks and stops it for the minor moving violation mentioned above. The officer intends not to enforce the minor moving violation but to conduct an investigatory stop of the vehicle because it just left a known drug house. This type of stop can lead to arrests for possessing illegal drugs, warrants, gun possession, etc.

A pretext stop is a powerful tool used almost exclusively to target criminal activity, the drug trade, and organized crime (gangs). Pretext stops help gather probable cause to submit a request for a search warrant or arrest warrant.

There is not much advice I can give someone stopped under these circumstances except to comply and not fight the officers who stopped you. Chances are you are not visiting your grandmother at a known drug house.

Investigatory Stops:

Investigatory stops do not involve traffic violations. These types of stops occur when a crime other than traffic violations has transpired, and the driver or occupants of the vehicle are suspects in those crimes.

Here is some example.

Officers respond to a domestic disturbance where an assault occurred. They receive additional information about a female victim who needs medical attention. The male suspect fled in a 2003 Red Chevy pickup truck. Within minutes, the officers arrived in the area and spotted the vehicle matching the description of the suspect vehicle. They stopped the vehicle, not for a traffic violation but because the driver was suspected of committing Family Violence.

The **P.A.S. Protocol©** applies to this type of stop.

Criminal Interdiction Stops:

Sometimes referred to as drug interdiction stops or interdiction stops, these stops are specific in their use, and the average citizen will rarely experience one. This type of stop targets drug trafficking, human trafficking, organized crime, and gang activity at border crossings and airports.

This type of stop relies on a criminal profile. Not to be confused with a racial profile (which is illegal), it utilizes common traits of, for example, drug traffickers to establish reasonable suspicion to conduct limited detentions of a person or a vehicle.

For example, at an international airport in any major American city, U.S. Customs agents are looking for travelers with one-way tickets from known drug trafficking locations such as Columbia, Mexico, Panama, etc. These individuals are usually young to middle age, male or female, and often very nervous when they notice law enforcement. If all or most of these indicators are present, a U.S. Customs agent can detain this individual to determine if they are a mule or a drug smuggler.

Another form of criminal interdiction is drug interdiction. This type of interdiction occurs on highways and interstates. Officers working in drug interdiction operations are looking for vehicles with telltale signs of drug trafficking. Some indicators can be rental cars from border towns in the U.S. or across the Mexican border. A vehicle that appears overloaded, riding like it is pulling a trailer without a trailer attached. License plate data indicates the vehicle recently crossed the U.S.-Mexican border. Confidential informant information that describes a specific vehicle will be on an interstate at a particular time carrying a load of narcotics.

Following the **P.A.S. Protocol©** is the best option during an interdiction stop.

Detentions:

Detentions differ from traffic stops because they often do not involve a traffic violation; they also use a lesser form of proof, known as reasonable suspicion. Detentions have various uses, such as investigating suspicious activity, interdicting criminals or criminal activity, preventing or reducing gang violence, and reasserting control of a high-crime area.

There is no universally accepted definition of a detention. Nevertheless, an officer may detain a person if the officer reasonably suspects that the person has committed, is committing, or is about to commit a crime.

Reasonable Suspicion:

Reasonable suspicion must be based on "articulable facts," "taken together with rational inferences from those facts," and the suspicion must be associated with the specific individual.

Within the definition of reasonable suspicion, we find the controversial topic of Terry Stops or the stop-and-frisk doctrine. These stops come from the court case Terry vs. Ohio.

That case permits officers to stop and briefly detain a person; when they have reasonable suspicion that a person has committed a crime, is in the process of committing a crime, or is about to commit a crime. It also allows for a frisk of the outer clothing of that person for weapons.

A frisk is not a search in the traditional sense of the word. A frisk is an act of feeling the outside of a pocket or area of a clothing item that could conceal a weapon to determine if there is a weapon present.

For example, when frisking an individual's pants pockets, if the officers can tell by the size, shape, or even weight that a handgun is concealed inside the pocket, they can reach into the pocket and remove the handgun. The same applies to pocket knives, brass knuckles, switchblades, etc.

Just because a person is detained for a crime or suspected crime does not automatically grant the officer the right to conduct a frisk. There has to be some articulation that leads the officer to reasonable suspicion that the person may be concealing a weapon.

The use of stop and frisk was most notable in New York City in recent years as a method to reduce gun violence. The program was successful because it resulted in the detection of illegally possessed weapons, reduced the number of murders annually, and resulted in more arrests of gang members. The controversy came when the statistics revealed that the vast majority of those stopped and frisked were minorities causing a backlash. New York City and many other cities later canceled the policy.

I do not intend to debate the merits of how the NYPD implemented stop and frisk. I use this example to illustrate how a stop-and-frisk policy works.

If you find yourself detained - for something other than a traffic violation - stay calm, be polite, ask questions respectfully, and remember that detentions are brief. The detention will end quickly unless additional evidence is uncovered. Be patient.

If you are frisked during a detention, stay calm and be polite. Remember, just like in traffic stops, officers in almost all states are required to wear body cameras. If there is wrongdoing by the officer, it will be more apparent if you are compliant and not aggressive.

Chapter 3 Arrests

An arrest is a method of charging a person with a crime.

For an arrest to occur, the proof necessary is probable cause. An arrest starts with handcuffing the person, followed by a search, and then transportation to a booking facility. A law enforcement officer then completes a booking sheet or report detailing the probable cause for arrest. An arraignment hearing then takes place within 24-48 hours. At an arraignment hearing, the arrested person can enter a plea, be granted or denied bail, and make a few phone calls to arrange bail or notify loved ones of where they are.

If arrested, here is what you should do:

1. **Comply** – do not resist (if the arrest is bad or illegal, there are ways to address the situation that do not involve violence or resistance).
2. **Be polite**, calm, and respectful – if an officer mistreats you, their behavior will be more prominent and seem more out of line if you are being respectful.
3. **Do not delay** the transport or booking process with fake medical emergencies, panic attacks, or other theatrics.
4. **Do not threaten** lawsuits, do not make threats toward the officers of physical violence because of the arrest, or threaten to get them fired. Making threats makes you the aggressor.
5. **Get bailed out**, contact an attorney, and, if necessary, file complaints for mistreatment (we will discuss complaints in a later chapter).

Comply, do not resist. If an officer makes an unlawful or illegal arrest, their actions will be clear if you are not resisting arrest.

Be polite, calm, and respectful. You are more likely to convince a jury, investigator, accountability board, or the public that you are innocent or a victim of police misconduct if you stay polite, calm, and respectful.

Do not delay your arrest with unreasonable requests, fake medical emergencies, or drama. Remember the **P.A.S. Protocol©** when we discussed signing the ticket to end the traffic stop quickly? The sooner the arrest is complete, the faster you will be eligible for bail and can go home.

Threatening lawsuits and threatening to assault the officer or their family make you the aggressor and unsympathetic. No one will believe you are innocent or a victim of police misconduct if you threaten to kill or assault a law enforcement officer or their family.

The sooner you get booked in, the sooner you can get to your arraignment and possibly secure bail. Additionally, you can make phone calls sooner to friends and family.

Arrest Procedure:

1. Manifestation of Arrest – you are told you are under arrest
2. Handcuffing – physically taking you into custody
3. Search – a search of your person
4. Transport – the ride to the jail
5. Booking – the end of the arrest process

Manifestation of Arrest:

In most situations, the officer will inform you of your arrest. For example, "you are under arrest for assault and family violence; put your hands behind your back." Alternatively, "put your hands behind your back; you are under arrest for assault and family violence."

At that moment, you have two choices:

1. Comply
2. Resist – <u>The worst possible choice, and I never recommend it.</u>

Complying is always the best choice, even if you feel the arrest is unwarranted, wrong, or illegal. There is a time and a place to question an arrest, but it is not during the arrest. Officers will respond quickly to any indication that a suspect is resisting. Verbally challenging the arrest could result in a resisting arrest or obstructing charge, so stay calm.

I mentioned that the second choice was resisting, but it was the worst choice. **It is incredibly dangerous to resist arrest and will likely result in**

you being injured and charged with additional crimes. It will also prevent you from mounting an effective defense if you are innocent.

Many people believe their Miranda rights must be read to them when arrested. That is a misconception. Miranda rights are only required if a law enforcement officer wants to question you about the crime you are under arrest for or any other crime you are suspected of committing.

Handcuffing:

Handcuffs are made of steel and are not comfortable. Officers can choose to handcuff someone in the front if they are physically disabled, but it is rare. Most suspects have their hands restrained behind their backs. Officers do not handcuff a suspect in the front of their body because it still allows the person the ability to fight, or use a weapon, so rarely are suspects handcuffed in front.

Search:

A search aims to locate weapons, contraband, and evidence. Unlike a frisk we discussed under detentions, this search is invasive, meaning they will check every part of your body for weapons or contraband (drugs). The officer will check your pockets, your clothes, waistband, etc.

Many suspects hate being searched, it is unpleasant to conduct or experience, but it is necessary and required before you can be transported and booked.

Transport:

Transporting a suspect to a jail or booking facility can vary. Some agencies utilize transport vehicles to take numerous suspects to jail at one time; other agencies require the arresting officer to transport the suspect themselves in a police vehicle.

Regardless of the method of transport, you will be assisted into the vehicle and seat belted in. The back seats of police vehicles are often molded plastic with a recessed area for your body to fit in. These types of backseats allow for a quick clean-up of bodily fluids. Unfortunately, they are very uncomfortable to ride in.

Do not do anything to delay your transport. Make the best of it, and hope
the ride is short.

Booking:

Booking is the completion of the arrest process for the law enforcement
officer. They will complete a booking form or report that includes a
probable cause statement supporting their arrest of the suspect. The
jailers will secure your property and return it to you upon release. You
may or may not be strip-searched. Every jail is different; some conduct
strip searches of every prisoner, and some do not.

After placing you in a holding cell, you will most likely see a judge at an
arraignment hearing within 24 – 48 hours. At that point, you may be
eligible for bail and can make additional phone calls. Do not resist the
officers who work in the jail or refuse to answer their questions; it can
make your stay longer and more uncomfortable.

Resisting Arrest and Why it is a Bad Idea:

Thousands of arrests take place every day in the United States. Most of
those arrests happen without the use of force by law enforcement officers
and occur peacefully.

However, a small percentage of those arrests involve the person resisting
arrest violently and sometimes to the point where deadly force is used.

<u>Choosing to resist arrest is a **Lose-Lose** proposition</u>.

The most common contributing factor to the death of someone in custody
by law enforcement is resisting arrest. Choosing to resist arrest, physically
fighting law enforcement officers, or attacking law enforcement officers
has a high likelihood of injury to the suspect and even death if the
suspect's actions threaten serious bodily injury or death.

Often, choosing to resist arrest is an impulsive decision.

The suspect's emotions (anger, fear, anxiety, etc.) play a role in the
decision to resist arrest. In addition, resisting arrest rarely achieves the
goal of escaping or pointing out injustice.

Resisting arrest, even if the suspect escapes custody, guarantees aggressive pursuit by law enforcement, increases the likelihood of force used against the suspect, and increases the criminal penalties for whatever crime the suspect committed.

Additionally, most officers wear body cameras to capture the suspect's actions, so resisting arrest is easy to prove.

Officers can use force equivalent to one level above the resistance or force used against them. For example, suppose a suspect chooses to fight an officer physically. In that case, the law enforcement officer can use an intermediate weapon such as pepper spray, Taser, baton, or A.S.P. baton to overcome the resistance or attack. Likewise, if a suspect attacks an officer with a baseball bat, two-by-four, shovel, or knife, the officer can use deadly force to protect themselves or another person.

Escalating force is why physical confrontations with law enforcement officers tend not to de-escalate until the suspect or attacker is subdued or can no longer attack.

Further, suppose you are a victim of police misconduct or excessive force. In that case, resisting arrest makes the decision of a jury, a police accountability board, or a police misconduct investigator less likely to be in your favor.

During my career, I have had many opportunities to ask suspects who resisted arrest why they did it. Most of the time, it was based on fear. They feared mistreatment by law enforcement, fear of returning to prison, and fear of losing their job, family, spouse, children, etc. However, many suspects said they did not want to go to jail. Sometimes the suspects said they did not know why they chose to resist but did it anyway.

In my experience, when suspects resisted violently and aggressively, they eventually became exhausted. Many suspects cannot continue to resist arrest due to an injury and give up because resisting an arrest requires extraordinary strength, endurance, and physical ability.

Let me use a hypothetical question to drive the point home about the foolish nature of choosing to resist arrest.

If I offered you a bet that you had a 100% chance of losing, which most likely would result in you being injured and increased the likelihood of a lengthy prison sentence, would you take that bet?

No rational person would take that bet. You would call me crazy for offering it.

Yet, everyday suspects take that unwinnable bet, sometimes betting their lives, when they resist arrest.

Do not take the bet. Stay alive and uninjured, so you can still be there for your family and friends.

Chapter 4 Complaints

No matter how many reforms to the law enforcement profession occur, officers will make mistakes, engage in misconduct, and even choose to break the law.

The men and women of the law enforcement profession have an ethical, moral, and legal duty to root out our fellow officers who willfully participate in misconduct and criminal behavior.

The purpose of this chapter is:

1. Understand the difference between mistakes, misconduct, and criminal behavior

2. To provide the reader with an understanding of how to file a complaint against a law enforcement officer

3. Understand how to use mediation as an alternative to filing a complaint

4. Having reasonable expectations of the outcomes of filing a complaint

Filing a formal complaint against a law enforcement officer is intimidating for most people. Many fear retaliation or do not believe it will make a difference.

You are not powerless if you are a victim of police misconduct, excessive force, or even criminal behavior committed by a law enforcement officer.

Knowing when to file a complaint, how to file a complaint, and what to expect can reduce the intimidation factor many citizens face.

Types of Complaints:

Generally, complaints against a law enforcement agency or law enforcement officers fall into three categories:

1. Service Complaints – a complaint about how services were rendered
2. Minor Complaints – low-level violations of policy or procedures
3. Major Complaints – serious misconduct such as excessive force, dereliction of duty, and criminal behavior.

Service Complaints: These are services you receive from your local law enforcement agency. They usually do not involve a specific officer. For example, a service complaint could be how long an officer took to arrive at a motor vehicle accident scene. Your concern is the time it took for emergency services to respond instead of the services you received once an officer was on the scene.

Minor Complaints: These are complaints about how officers behaved or conducted themselves. A rudeness complaint is a minor complaint. A minor complaint does not result in significant discipline most of the time. Retraining, written reprimands, and possibly a one-day suspension are common remedies for confirmed minor complaints.

Major Complaints: These are critical concerns taken seriously by those entrusted to investigate them. Excessive force complaints, violating an individual's civil rights, are within this category of complaints. These complaints can result in termination, multi-day suspensions, demotions, and criminal charges.

The vast majority of complaints filed against law enforcement officers are minor complaints. Most of those minor complaints involve behavior that violates a policy or procedure of the police agency.

Every police agency, no matter how big or small, will have a policy manual – sometimes called rules and regulations, procedures manual, or departmental guidelines – these documents instruct law enforcement officers on how to perform their job and prohibit behavior.

For example, most policy manuals will have a Code of Conduct section. A Code of Conduct section details unacceptable behaviors. Examples of those behaviors are:

1. Sleeping on duty
2. Unprofessional Behavior
3. Insubordination
4. Conflicts of Interest
5. Recommending Attorneys or Businesses
6. Dereliction of Duty
7. Poor Performance
8. Conduct Unbecoming

It is essential to understand that every sworn officer at a law enforcement agency must know and follow the policies and procedures of their agency. Failure to follow those policies and procedures is a violation, resulting in discipline.

Commonly, discipline falls along the lines of severity and culpability. Some agencies use letters or numbers to denote severity (A through F), A being the least serious and F being the most serious. Alternatively, one being the most serious and six being the least serious. Some agencies use classes of violations, such as Class 1 or Class 2.

Culpability is an area where many people need clarification. If a law enforcement officer violates their department's policy, the investigator will assign a culpable mental state to the violation.

Here are examples of culpability:

1. Intentionally – The officer intended with forethought to commit the violation
2. Knowingly – The officer knew what they were doing was prohibited
3. Recklessly – The officer disregarded the policy without concern for the consequences
4. Negligently – The officer was careless or did not comprehend that their actions were prohibited
5. Inexperience – The officer may be so new or inexperienced that they did not think they had committed a violation

The officer who commits the violation does not set their culpability; the investigator, or in some cases, the Chief or Sheriff, determines their culpability.

Many Law enforcement agencies have labor contracts that limit the discipline a law enforcement officer can receive. In addition, many municipal governments and some counties are large enough to qualify for civil service protections for their police and fire departments. Depending on your state, those civil service protections can further reduce the discipline an employee can receive.

Mistakes vs. Misconduct:

Mistakes:

I took many complaints from citizens over the years who needed clarification on the difference between mistakes versus misconduct. It is essential to realize that law enforcement officers are human, and human error occurs in every profession.

Human error is preventable to a degree but cannot be eliminated.

Nevertheless, mistakes or human errors can result from poor training and ineffective decision-making. It is also important to point out that those mistakes or human errors are not intentional acts but a result of negligence or inexperience.

It is necessary to understand that heads do not need to roll if a law enforcement officer makes a minor mistake. If every law enforcement officer were suspended or fired for making a minor mistake, no one would want to become a law enforcement officer.

Having the proper viewpoint will help you know when to file a complaint or instead speak with a supervisor to get the error corrected.

For example, complaints about spelling errors in a report are not misconduct and do not require discipline. Yet, many citizens demand the firing or suspension of the officer for these errors.

The best course of action is to speak with the officer's supervisor and have the errors corrected.

Misconduct:

Misconduct is behavior that is unprofessional, unethical, immoral, or not an accepted police practice.

Misconduct has categories of severity and requires a culpable mental state.

For example, it is widely accepted that if a law enforcement officer lied on a governmental document (police report, arrest report, citation, etc.), that violation always results in immediate termination.

Conversely, if a law enforcement officer is rude or unprofessional to a citizen, that violation is not always a termination-level offense. It could result in retraining, a letter of reprimand, or suspension.

Allegations of misconduct can lead to criminal charges against a law enforcement officer, so it is crucial to get it right if you file a complaint for misconduct.

Criminal Behavior:

Criminal behavior in the line of duty is unacceptable.

Corrupt officers who violate an individual's civil rights, use excessive force, steal from others, use their position for economic gain, or join criminal organizations; have no place In law enforcement.

An officer accused of criminal behavior will usually have that behavior investigated by an outside law enforcement agency. For example, in Texas, the Texas Rangers investigate public corruption cases involving police officers, judges, elected officials, and public servants.

Knowing when misconduct is criminal or not is essential to understand. Suppose you feel you are a victim of criminal behavior committed by a police officer. In that case, you should retain or hire an attorney specializing in public corruption or civil rights violations and rely on their advice. Then go, for example, to the F.B.I., or state agency investigating those types of crimes.

How to File a Complaint:

Filing a misconduct complaint against a police officer or law enforcement officer can be intimidating and confusing.

The maxim that "information is power" is true. Knowing what to expect during the complaint process will give you the confidence to know when and how to file a complaint.

Before you file a complaint, you need to know how the process works.

1. You must have legal standing to file a complaint
2. Hearsay and third-party information are not allowed
3. Most agencies require you to sign the complaint and tell the truth
4. Witnesses must be direct witnesses
5. Evidence – the best evidence is police body camera or in-car camera footage
6. Offering to take a polygraph exam is an option
7. You may be required to testify at an arbitration

Legal Standing:

Legal Standing is a term that refers to a person's ability to bring legal action; for example, most agencies will only allow a person who was a victim of police misconduct to file a complaint. This means that you cannot file a complaint on behalf of another person unless that person is a minor and only if you are the parent or guardian of the minor. If the victim is disabled, a caretaker can file a complaint on their behalf.

Hearsay:

You cannot file a complaint based on hearsay or third-party information. You must have first-hand knowledge about the misconduct.

Writing the Complaint and Signing Complaints:

Being truthful when filing a complaint is critical. More so than any other type of communication, such as text messages, email, and social media posts, accuracy is the number one priority when completing a complaint. Refrain from expressing opinions, feelings, or what you think happened or assigning blame.

Only detail what you directly experienced during the incident. Making assumptions about an officer's motivation is also a non-starter. For example, many victims of police misconduct want to claim that the reason for the misconduct was racial bias. It could be that it is, but unless you can prove it, claiming it only muddies the water. Let the investigator conclude that racial discrimination occurred based on the facts, not assumptions.

Your goal in filing a complaint is to make clear that you were mistreated, that the action or actions of the officer were unwarranted, and how the result of those actions affected you.

The results side of your complaint is where you can describe what you felt and experienced. Be clear and descriptive. For example, it was humiliating when the officer cursed at me and called me a crackhead. Or, after the officer assaulted me unlawfully, I suffered physical pain, swelling, and bruising."

Most Law enforcement agencies will require you to sign the complaint under penalty of perjury. Many complaint forms will have a statement before or after the signature informing you of the penalty of perjury if you are untruthful. Tell the truth, and sign the form. If you refuse to sign the complaint, an investigation will likely not occur.

Witnesses:

Many complaints want to bring witnesses when filing a complaint. Listing your witnesses in the complaint and letting the investigator interview them separately is better. It is essential to define what a witness is because it can be confusing. Many victims of police misconduct believe that if you tell someone about the misconduct or they hear about it, they are a witness. You will be wasting your time if you claim those individuals are witnesses.

Witnesses must be physically present at the incident and directly observe some or all of the misconduct you experienced.

The credibility of the witnesses is essential. Generally, you cannot choose the witnesses to an incident, but knowing their background is critical. For example, suppose the only witnesses you have are gang members with a documented history of assaulting officers, violent offenses, perjury, or fraud. In that case, an investigator will be less inclined to view them as credible.

The best type of witness is an independent third-party witness. Independent third-party witnesses are not family members, friends, or people you know. They often are people you have never met and therefore have no incentive to be untruthful or deceptive.

Only get their contact information if you know of an independent third-party witness to police misconduct. Do not speak with them about the misconduct. Doing so could lead an investigator to believe you influenced the witness in a biased way toward your version of events.

Evidence:

In today's society, people will only believe an incident happened if there is video evidence. However, there are varying degrees of video evidence, and it is essential to understand the difference.

Cellphone footage is typical in police misconduct cases. Still, the problem with this type of evidence is that manipulation is possible, and the person who took it must withstand credibility challenges. If it is all you got, use it.

Police body camera and in-car camera footage is the best evidence if you can get it. For example, if there are pending charges, then the footage is evidence and is not releasable. However, the police misconduct investigator can access the footage, so note that the officer or officers were wearing body cameras in your complaint.

Polygraph Exams:

It is rare nowadays, but some law enforcement agencies do not have body cameras or in-car cameras. In those instances, unless you have cellphone footage, it will be your word against the officer's word. One way to level the playing field is to offer to take a polygraph exam.

A word of caution, polygraph exams are not admissible in court for a reason. Their accuracy is somewhere around 70 percent.

If you choose this route, insist the officer take a polygraph exam. However, be warned; it can backfire on you. For example, your test results could indicate deception or be inconclusive, yet you are still telling the truth. It is a gamble but still an option.

Arbitration:

If the officer violated their department's policy, based on your complaint, the result is discipline. Some forms of punishment are appealable such as suspensions and terminations. Suppose the officer appeals the punishment, then an arbitrator who acts as an independent assessor (like a judge) comes in to review the case. Sometimes an arbitrator will issue a ruling based on their review, but often will hold a hearing where both sides present evidence and call witnesses, and the arbitrator acts as judge and jury.

During the arbitration, you will have to testify. It is important to note that these types of hearing are adversarial. You will be cross-examined, and your version of events challenged. The lawyer for the city or country that suspended or terminated the officer will represent you. Tell the truth, avoid unprovable statements, and stay calm.

Be realistic about the potential outcome. Appeals to arbitration seek to overturn the discipline, modify or change it, or reduce it. Both sides commonly will compromise before the arbitration, and there is no need for a hearing. Those compromises could be reinstatement if the officer were terminated, reduced suspension time (from ten days to five days), or even dismissal of the discipline entirely.

Mediation (optional):

Filing a complaint is a long and stressful endeavor. There may be a better course of action in some cases. Mediation is a good alternative for minor misconduct, such as rudeness or unprofessional behavior.

Mediation is an informal process where both sides are present (officer and victim), discussing what happened and offering opportunities for reconciliation. The Chief of Police, Sheriff, police misconduct investigator, or the officer's supervisor often mediates these situations.

I utilized mediation several times in my career and found it helpful.

The essential part of mediation is the victim's ability to tell the officer how their actions made them feel. During this part of the mediation, many officers change their attitude based on the victim's statements and offer an apology for their actions.

Mediation detaches the officer from the heat of the moment, gets them out of their official capacity where they expect compliance, and helps them see the real pain they can inflict with their attitude or choice of words.

It can be helpful if you are willing to try mediation for minor police misconduct.

Reasonable Expectations:

When you file a complaint against a law enforcement officer, remember that they get to defend themselves. Many states have laws that protect law enforcement officers from frivolous or false complaints. Additionally, some states have due process rights for law enforcement officers.

Every story has two sides; a good police misconduct investigator will examine both sides and follow the evidence.

The burden of proof in police misconduct cases (not criminal cases) is a preponderance of the evidence. The best description of the legal standard of preponderance is 51 percent probability.

That is a lower threshold than beyond a reasonable doubt, but it is a challenging burden to meet.

Filing a complaint is not a guarantee that the outcome you desire will occur. Police misconduct rarely happens in a vacuum where the behavior is clear-cut and wrong.

Be realistic, understand the process, and tell the truth. Even if you do not get what you think you deserve, your complaint could reveal a behavior pattern leading to accountability later.

Why Filing a Complaint Matters:

Medium, large, and metropolitan-sized law enforcement agencies employ hundreds, even thousands of law enforcement officers. Officers who work in those agencies have minimal direct contact with their supervisors.

Those supervisors have too many administrative duties and do not spend enough time observing their subordinates in the field.

Many law enforcement supervisors report that the only way they knew a subordinate had committed misconduct was from complaints filed by citizens. Those complaints can reveal patterns of behavior such as chronic unprofessionalism, excessive force usage, or criminal behavior that would have gone undetected.

Filing a complaint for misconduct can also lead to mental health services for law enforcement officers in crisis. There is strong circumstantial evidence of a link between excessive force complaints and repeated exposure to the emotional trauma that law enforcement officers experience during their careers. Other police misconduct can be an outcry for help by an officer who does not know how to deal with the pressures and stresses of the profession.

If a misconduct investigation leads to a diagnosis of a mental health crisis, it often results in treatment for the officer. A mental health crisis does not remove accountability for the actions of the officer involved but is part of determining the origins of the misconduct.

Do not discount making a minor misconduct complaint. It can lead to more accountability than just your complaint and help officers in crisis get the assistance they need.

Final Thoughts

The theme of this book was to open a window into police culture and to give you an understanding of how to interact with law enforcement officers safely and effectively. Educate the public about traffic stops, detentions, and arrests. Inform the public about the dangers of resisting arrest. Also, empower citizens to know when and how to file a police misconduct complaint.

If you take only one helpful thing from this book, follow and tell others about the **P.A.S. Protocol©.**

P.A.S. – Protocol©

P – Pull to the right and stop (stay in your vehicle unless directed out by the officer)

A – Avoid confrontation, don't argue, insult, or accuse, and stay polite

S – Sign the citation or ticket to end the traffic stop quickly

If you are still fearful of police encounters by the end of this book, then try meeting enforcement officers in non-official situations. Community events such as National Night Out and civic events are great ways to meet law enforcement officers in non-enforcement situations. Those events allow law enforcement officers to interact with the public in low-stress environments, resulting in greater understanding between the community and law enforcement.

Finally, thank you, the reader, for taking the time to read this book. It has been many years in the making and is more relevant now than ever. If you like this book, tell others and spread the word.

May God bless you and keep you safe.

Timothy Weston